FIRST BOOK OF SCIENCE

Gaby Waters

Designed and illustrated by
Graham Round

Contents
Part 1

Science consultant: Julie Fitzpatrick

About this section

This section contains lots of fun science experiments for you to try.

Some of them are noisy and several are quite messy. There are even some experiments to eat and drink. They all produce surprising and unexpected results.

Meet the monster gang

Each experiment has been tried and tested by the monster gang. They will guide you through each one, step by step.

You can meet the main members of the gang who appear in this section, on the right.

Micky MacMonster, the leader of the monster gang.

Clutty Putty. She is very fond of messy experiments.

Cloth Ears. He is more sneaky than he looks, so watch out.

1 On page 30 there are some extra, more detailed explanations.

As you do each experiment, you can find out how and why it works. You can also discover the science behind all sorts of everyday things.

2

The experiments are completely safe and use ordinary ingredients that you can find at home.

3

Cardboard tubes

Plastic containers

Jam jars

Empty bottles

For science equipment, you can use everyday things like these. On page 32 there are some ideas for making a science kit.

Horace Hogwash, called Hogwash for short.

Slimy Sid and his Aunty Mabel from Australia.

Normus Noze   Snivel   Parsifal P. Brain

There are lots of other monsters as well.

The Gruesome twins, Fester and Blot

Making frosty patterns

Surprise your friends by covering your bedroom window with these frosty patterns. They look like real frost, but you can even make them on a boiling hot day.

Hogwash is holding the list of things you need. Find out how to make the frost below.

THINGS YOU NEED

MIXING BOWL
SPONGE
CUP
SPOON
WASHING SODA *
HOT WATER (from the tap)

How to make the frost

1 When the crystals disappear they become part of the liquid. In other words, they "dissolve".

Put a cup of washing soda crystals into the bowl, then pour in about the same amount of hot water. Stir them together until most of the crystals disappear.

2 You can wipe the window in any direction, but try not to go over the same bit twice.

Dip the sponge into the liquid and wipe it on to a window. Leave it for about 20 minutes and wait to see what happens.

3 Be careful with food colouring. It can stain things.

To make the frost look icier, add two dessert spoons of blue food colouring to the liquid. Try using other colours as well and see what the frost looks like.

4   *You can buy washing soda in most supermarkets, grocers and hardware stores.

Why the frosty patterns appear

You can wipe the frost off the window with a damp cloth.

As the liquid dries on the window, the water disappears into the air. This leaves the crystals, looking like frost, stuck to the window. The crystals are no longer in big lumps. Now they are spread thinly over the surface of the window.

*You can buy Epsom salts in a chemists shop.

Something to try

You can also frost the windows with bath crystals or Epsom salts.* The patterns may be different. Try them and see.

What is a crystal?

Crystals are solid substances with a regular shape. Lots of things are crystals. Some are shown below.

Sugar

SAND

SALT

Precious stones such as diamonds and rubies

When water contains dissolved crystals it is called a solution.

See if you can find out which of these crystals dissolve in hot water. You can check your results on page 32.

Then try changing them back into crystals by leaving them in a warm place, so the water dries up.

Sea salt crystals

The sea is a solution because it contains dissolved salt. After a swim on a hot day, you sometimes find salt crystals on your skin. The water dries up, leaving the salt behind.

Fizzing and foaming

On these two pages, Micky and the monster gang are mixing ordinary, everyday ingredients to produce fantastic fizzy results. You can do the same. Start with a frothy explosion by making Clutty Putty's bursting bottle.

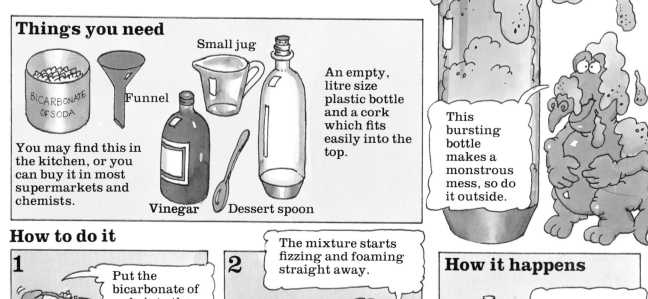

Things you need

Funnel

Small jug

Vinegar

Dessert spoon

BICARBONATE OF SODA

You may find this in the kitchen, or you can buy it in most supermarkets and chemists.

An empty, litre size plastic bottle and a cork which fits easily into the top.

This bursting bottle makes a monstrous mess, so do it outside.

How to do it

1 Put the bicarbonate of soda into the bottle through the funnel.

Put 4 dessert spoons of bicarbonate of soda into the bottle. Then measure out 10 dessert spoons of vinegar into the jug.

2 The mixture starts fizzing and foaming straight away.

Pour the vinegar into the bottle and quickly push in the cork. Stand well back and wait for the explosion.

How it happens

You can see tiny bubbles of gas in the foam.

When you mix vinegar and bicarbonate of soda they produce a gas, called carbon dioxide. The gas foams and escapes, pushing out the cork with a pop.

Other ways of making carbon dioxide gas

ACIDS
DESSERT SPOON OF LIME JUICE
JUICE OF HALF AN ORANGE
JUICE OF 1 LEMON
2 CRUSHED GRAPES

CARBONATES
4 LUMPS OF WASHING SODA
TEASPOON OF BAKING POWDER
SMALL PIECE OF LIMESTONE, CHALK OR MARBLE
CRUSHED EGG SHELL

You can mix other things to make carbon dioxide gas. Choose something from each list in this picture and mix them in a jam jar. They will foam and fizz as the carbon dioxide gas escapes.

The ingredients on the left contain a substance called acid. Those on the right are called carbonates. Whenever you mix an acid with a carbonate they make carbon dioxide gas.

Making sherbert fizz

1 MICKY'S SPECIAL SHERBERT MIX
2 SPOONS OF CITRIC ACID CRYSTALS*
1 SPOON OF BICARBONATE OF SODA
6 SPOONS OF ICING SUGAR

Sherbert powder fizzes because it contains an acid and a carbonate. Try making sherbert yourself by mixing up all the ingredients in Micky's recipe.

Inside Slimy Sid's mouth the citric acid crystals dissolve and mix with the bicarbonate of soda. This produces bubbles of carbon dioxide that make the fizzy feeling.

The bubbles in fizzy drinks are made of carbon dioxide. Make your own drinks fizzy by adding sherbert powder. Put 2 tablespoons of sherbert into each drink.

*You can buy citric acid crystals in a chemists shop.

Wind power

The monster gang are racing their home-made land yachts. The yachts run on wind power, in other words they are pushed by the wind. It's surprising how fast they can move.

Find out how the monsters made their land-yacht below and see if you can improve on their design.

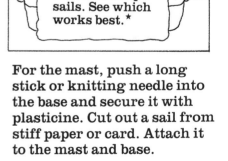

Making a land yacht

1

You may need to cut the polystyrene to the right size.

2

Stick a blob of plasticine on the pointed ends to stop the reels flying off.

Make sure the wheels spin freely. For extra spin, try oiling the needles.

3

Experiment with different shape sails. See which works best.*

For the base you can use a block of polystyrene. This is used for ceiling tiles and packing things. The base of Slimy Sid's yacht is 20cm long and 15cm wide.

For the wheels, thread cotton reels on to both ends of two knitting needles. Attach the needles to the base with sticky tape.

For the mast, push a long stick or knitting needle into the base and secure it with plasticine. Cut out a sail from stiff paper or card. Attach it to the mast and base.

8   *Clutty Putty has made a square sail. You could try a triangular one, like the sails on real yachts.

The wind at work

As the wind moves, it pushes things around. It is so good at doing this that it is used as a source of power to make things move and work.

The wind fills the sails of boats and wind-surfers and makes them move, just like your land-yacht.

The wind pushes the sails of a windmill round and round. This drives the machine inside the mill.

4

The yachts work best on a windy day, but you can make your own wind, like this.

Now give your yacht a test run. Don't worry if it doesn't sail perfectly at first. You may need to make improvements, especially to the mast and sail.

Problems with wind power

The problem with wind as a source of power is that it is unreliable. Boats were sometimes stuck on a calm sea with no wind for days and days.

Spinning and whirling

Guess what happens when Clutty Putty swings a bucket round and round in the air.

Try it yourself and see. Half fill a small bucket with water then spin it as fast as you can.

Do this outside in waterproof clothes, just in case.

The water stays in the bucket.

Why the water stays in the bucket

As you spin the bucket, the water is pushed outwards. The bottom of the bucket stops the water going any further, so the water sticks to the bottom of the bucket.

Look below to find out more about the force that pushes the water outwards.

Outward force in action

Micky puts ping-pong balls on his monster-disc turntable. The movement of the spinning turntable pushes the balls outwards. There is nothing to stop them, so they fly off.

At the fair

You can see the outward force working at a fairground. Some of the rides that use it are shown

The same outward force holds the rollercoaster to the rails when it loops the loop.

in this picture. Next time you go the fair, see if you can spot some others.

The outward force pushes you against the wall of this roundabout. It is so strong that you stick to the wall and don't need to hold on.

As the roundabout whirls around, the space rockets are pushed outwards. The rockets are attached to chains to stop them flying away.

Drying things

Spinning and whirling can remove water from wet things and make them dry. A spin-dryer whirls wet clothes round and round in a drum. The water is pushed outwards and escapes through holes in the drum.

In a salad dryer, the salad spins round in a plastic container. The water is pushed out through holes in the container.

How to make Aunty Mabel's salad spinner

Slimy Sid's Aunty Mabel made a salad spinner with an empty slime sorbet tub and a piece of string about 150cm long. You can use any sort of plastic container.

1

Ask someone to help you make holes in the bottom and sides of the tub.

2

Tie knots here to secure the string.

Attach the string to the tub to make a long handle.

3

Do this outside or you won't be very popular.

Put some washed salad in the tub and swing it round and round in the air.

Soapy straw surprises

Have a go at the surprising soapy straw trick below. First find the equipment that the monsters are collecting, on the right.

Like them, you will need a bowl of cold water, 4 matches, a bar of soap and a drinking straw.

1 Float the matches on the water in a star shape, as shown above.

2 Then rub some soap on to the end of the straw.

3 Dip the soapy straw into the water in the centre of the matches. See what happens.

What is happening?

The surface of the water is like a skin. Soap makes a hole in the skin and pushes it away to the edge of the bowl. The matches move with the skin.

You can find out more about water's skin on the opposite page.

Water's skin

The skin on the surface of water is caused by a force called surface tension.

You can see surface tension in action if you fill a cup with water. Do it very gently and you can make the water level rise higher than the cup without it overflowing. Surface tension holds it in place.

Surface tension makes water dripping from a tap form into droplets. Water droplets are firm and round because their skin holds them together.

Droplet squashing game

1

2

Washing things

Put some drops of water on a table, just like Micky. Dip a clean straw in water, put your finger over the top and lift it out. Take your finger away and the water will drop out.

Now touch the droplets with the soapy straw. See how they spread out and go flat. This happens because soap makes the surface tension weaker and breaks the water's skin.

Water is attracted to soap more than it is attracted to itself. This is why soap reduces surface tension. Soap is also attracted to dirt and grease. It sticks to the grease on the plates and water pulls the grease and soap off.

Tasting tests

In the pictures below, Cloth Ears is doing a tricky taste test on his good friend Normus Noze. Find a trusting friend to help and you can try these taste tests too. Be prepared for some very unexpected results.

Apple or potato?

1

First, Cloth Ears grates some raw apple and potato on to separate plates.

2

Then he gets Normus Noze to block his nose, shut his eyes and open his mouth.

3

Try it yourself. It's really tricky to tell which is which.

He puts a spoonful of apple or potato into Normus Noze's mouth and asks him to guess which it is.

What is happening?

Your tongue can only detect basic tastes. You use your sense of smell to work out the flavours of foods. When your nose is blocked, it is hard to taste the flavour of the food in your mouth.

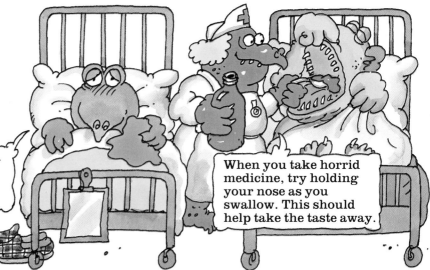

You card daste dings bery well when you hab a code and your doze iz blockd.

When you take horrid medicine, try holding your nose as you swallow. This should help take the taste away.

14

Tongue map

Your tongue can detect four basic tastes. These are bitter, sweet, salty and sour. Different parts of the tongue can taste different things.

This picture of Cloth Ears' tongue shows the different taste areas. The areas overlap a bit in most people (and some monsters).

Tongue testing

It tastes sweetest on the tip of my tongue.

Try testing the taste areas of your tongue. Put some sugar in different places on your tongue. Where can you taste it best?

You may not taste bitter things until you swallow as the bitter taste area is at the back.

Do the same with something bitter (strong black coffee), salty (yeast extract or salty water), and sour (vinegar).

Using your eyes

Your eyes also help you taste food. Have a go at the experiments below. You will be surprised how hard it is to taste food when you cannot see it.

Pour out a glass each of grapefruit and orange juice. Blindfold yourself, shuffle the glasses and drink them in turn. Can you tell the difference between them?

Mystery fruit test

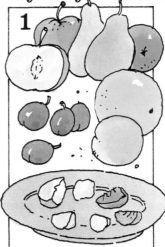

1

2

?

Cut a bite size chunk out of several different fruits, like the ones in this picture.

Blindfold a friend and give him each chunk in turn. Can he tell you which is which?

15

Static surprises

Micky and the monster gang have discovered some snappy experiments to impress their rivals, the Roughcut Reptiles. Try them out. You will find that strange, almost magic things will happen.

Micky's pool of piranhas

Give them gaping jaws and sharp teeth so they look like piranha fish.

Cut out 20 to 30 paper fish, each about 3cm long. Put them in a plastic container with a transparent lid.*

Rub a plastic ruler with a woolly scarf quite briskly for about 10 seconds.

Slide the ruler across the lid. Watch the piranha fish jump from the bottom of their "pool" up to the lid.

Sticky surprises

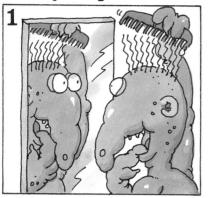

The monster moves towards the comb as if it is sitting up.

Comb your hair very fast. Hold the comb above your head and look in a mirror to see what happens.

Rub a plastic spoon with a woolly scarf and hold it near a trickle of water. The water bends towards the spoon.

Cut out a tissue paper monster. Rub a plastic ruler on your sleeve and hold it over the monster's head.

*Micky used a mould-flavour mousse container, but you could use an empty margarine tub.

What is happening?

All these experiments happen because of static electricity. Static electricity is not the same as electricity you use at home. You can make it by rubbing things together, as shown below.

> These uncharged scraps of paper are attracted to the balloon and stick to it.

> Plastic and nylon hold static electricity better than other substances.

When you rub something it becomes "charged" with static electricity. When something is charged with static electricity, it pulls or "attracts" things that are not charged, like the scraps of paper in this picture.

Crackles and sparks

Clutty Putty is tap dancing in plastic-soled clodhoppers. She rubs her feet on the carpet, then touches a metal radiator. Do this yourself. You may feel a tiny shock of static electricity running through your body.

Feeling static

When you undress, you can sometimes hear crackling noises. If it's dark, you may even see tiny sparks. This is static electricity made by your clothes rubbing together.

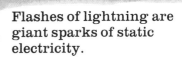

Flashes of lightning are giant sparks of static electricity.

17

Buzzy bee balloon

The buzzy bee balloon whizzes round and round in the air, making a loud buzzing noise. Hogwash and Micky show you how to make it.

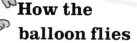

How to make a buzzy bee balloon

1

Long, sausage shape balloons work best.

For the bee's body the monsters use a yellow balloon. Micky draws black stripes all over it and adds two blobs for eyes. Hogwash cuts out tissue paper wings. He makes them quite big so they are the right size when the balloon is blown up.

2

Use tiny bits of sticky tape to attach the wings.

Then they blow up the balloon. Hogwash holds the end tight and Micky sticks on the wings.

3

You can blow up the balloon and make it fly again and again.

Let go of the balloon and watch the bee buzz about. It will whizz around until all the air inside it has gone.

How the balloon flies

Scientists describe the way the balloon flies as "action and reaction". This means that movement in one direction causes movement in the opposite direction.

The buzzing noise is the air rushing out of the balloon.

When you let go of the balloon, the air rushes backwards out of it. This causes a reaction which pushes the balloon forwards.

Did you know?

Rockets and jets work in the same way. Hot gases rush out backwards. This pushes them forwards.

P. P. Brain's flinging machine

You can see "action and reaction" at work in Parsifal P. Brain's new invention, the flinging machine. You will need a grown-up to help you make it.

You can find these in the middle of a roll of kitchen towel.

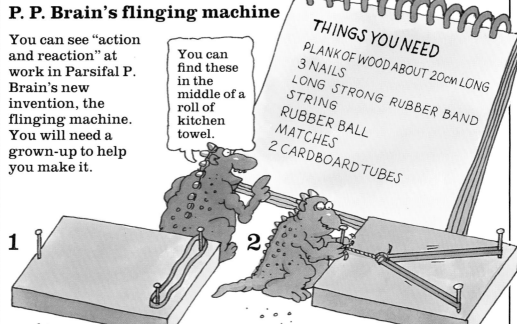

THINGS YOU NEED
PLANK OF WOOD ABOUT 20cm LONG
3 NAILS
LONG STRONG RUBBER BAND
STRING
RUBBER BALL
MATCHES
2 CARDBOARD TUBES

1

First ask someone to bang the nails into the wood, as shown above. Hook the rubber band round the two nails at one end.

2

Tie the string to the rubber band. Pull it so the rubber band is stretched back, almost to the third nail. Tie the string to the nail.

3

Balance the plank on the tubes, and put the ball in front of the rubber band. Then get a grown-up to burn the string with a match. Stand back and watch.

4

The string breaks and releases the rubber band. The ball is hurled across the room. This causes a reaction in the opposite direction and the plank rolls backwards.

19

Airy surprises

Did you know that air can squash a bottle?

If you don't believe it, try Micky's bottle squashing experiment below.

Micky's amazing bottle squasher

1 Fill the bottle up to about this level.

Pour very hot water from the tap into an empty bottle made of soft plastic.

2

Let the steam shoot out of the bottle and screw the top on quickly. See what happens.

How the bottle is squashed

Air presses down on us all the time. This is called air pressure and it squashes the bottle.

The steam pushes out most of the air.

The air outside presses against the bottle. There is almost no air inside to push against it so it crushes the bottle.

The undrinkable drink

Cloth Ears is preparing a sneaky surprise for his friends.

Press in the plasticine tightly and make sure there are no gaps.

He fills a bottle to the brim with orange ooze and puts a straw in it. Then he pushes plasticine into the bottle neck as a stopper.

Can trick

1

SLIME JUICE

Find a can of fruit juice and make a small hole in it, as Snivel has done.

20

Try removing the plasticine. The air can get in and you can have a drink.

The pressure of the air gets weaker the higher you are.

POP   POP

Now he offers his friends a refreshing slurp. But, however hard they try, they cannot suck up more than a tiny drop. The plasticine stops the air getting into the bottle. You cannot suck up the drink unless there is air pushing down on it to help it up the straw.

If you gain height quickly, you can sometimes feel your ears popping. This happens because the pressure of the outside air is different from the air in your ears.

2

The air pushes up and stops the juice coming out.

Turn the can upside down and see if you can pour out the contents.

3

The air gets in through one hole and pushes the slime out through the other one.

Now make another hole and try pouring out the fruit juice.

You can stop the popping by yawning. This lets outside air into your ears and makes the pressure inside and outside equal.

Amazing liquids

Clutty Putty's special multi-colour cocktail contains three exotic ingredients in separate layers.

Try making it yourself following Clutty's recipe, below. The ingredients are listed on the right.

INGREDIENTS
FIZZY DRINK
FRUIT SYRUP SUCH AS
BLACKCURRANT CORDIAL
3 TABLESPOONS OF CREAM
COLOURED WITH FOOD DYE

Clutty Putty's cocktail recipe

Don't stir the drink!

Fill a glass with fizzy drink. Clutty Putty's favourite is fizzy melonade. Then pour in enough syrup or cordial to cover the bottom of the glass. Add the coloured cream very gently, one spoon at a time.

Why is the drink in layers?

Density is a word scientists use for comparing weights of different things.

The drink is layered because the ingredients have different weights, or "densities". The syrup sinks to the bottom because it is denser, or heavier than the fizzy drink. Cream is lighter, or less dense, so it stays on the top.

Density test

COOKING OIL

FRUIT CORDIAL

MAPLE SYRUP

MILK

TREACLE

ORANGE JUICE

Can you find out which of these liquids are denser than water and which are less dense? Drop a spoonful of each one into a jar of water and see if it sinks or floats. Check your results on page 32.

Bottle fountain

Now try making a coloured bottle fountain. The Gruesome twins, Fester and Blot, show you how to do it, below.

First the twins find two identical bottles. Fester fills one with cold tap water coloured with food dye. Blot and his friend fill the other one with salty water. To make salty water, you mix three tablespoons of salt in a jug of hot water and leave it to cool.

Fester puts a piece of card over the top of the salty water bottle. He holds the card tight, turns the bottle

upside down and balances it on the other bottle. Blot holds the two bottles and Fester removes the card gently.

The coloured tap water rises because it is less dense than salty water.

You may be able to see some water moving downwards. This is the dense, salty water sinking to the bottom.

Did you know?

Things float more easily in dense (heavy) liquids. This is why it is easier to swim in the sea. The salty water is denser than ordinary water so it helps to keep you afloat.

The Dead Sea in the Middle East is extra salty, so it is very easy to float in it.

Crazy colours

You can make these amazing patterns with your coloured felt pens. The only other things you need are a saucer of water and blotting paper. You can buy this in most stationers shops.

How to make the patterns

1

Write your name on blotting paper using a different coloured felt pen for each letter.

2

Dip the bottom of the paper in the saucer of water. Leave it for a few minutes and watch the patterns appear.

Why the patterns appear

Dark colours, like this, contain more chemicals than others.

Different colours make different patterns.

The inks in your felt pens are made from a mixture of different coloured chemicals. The water rises up the blotting paper taking these chemicals with it.

Different chemicals travel at different speeds and so the colours separate, making patterns. Separating chemicals like this is called chromatography.

Surprising black ink

Black ink is made from lots of different chemicals. These vary with different makes of pen. Try doing some chromatography tests with several different black pens, as Micky is doing below.

1 Label each test strip with pencil so you know which pen made which blob.

Cut several strips of blotting paper and mark each one with a black blob 3cm from the bottom. Use black fountain pen ink and different black felt pens.

2 The colours vary and separate in different ways for each black blob.

Put the strips into a jam jar filled with about 2cm of water. In a few minutes the water separates the different chemicals in each black ink.

3 Shut your eyes tight so you can't see which pen is used.

The monster gang use these chromatography strips for detective work. Slimy Sid writes a mystery message on blotting paper in black pen. Hogwash shuts his eyes.

4

MEET ME AT MIDNIGHT

I can tell which pen Slimy Sid used by the way the colours separate.

Hogwash dips the paper in water. When the colours separate, he compares the result with the test strips to find out which pen was used to write the message.

Things to try

You can do chromatography tests on all sorts of things that contain coloured inks or dyes. Some things work better than others. Try them and see.

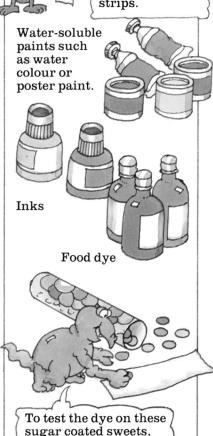

Do the chromatography tests on blotting paper strips.

Water-soluble paints such as water colour or poster paint.

Inks

Food dye

To test the dye on these sugar coated sweets, lick them and dab them on the paper.

Sounds surprising

The monster gang are doing some fun experiments with sounds and noises. See what they are doing and try them yourself. Get ready for some strange and surprising sounds.

Spoon Bells

1

Cut a piece of string about a metre long. Then tie it to a small metal spoon as Cloth Ears is doing.

2

Hold the ends of the string to your ears. Then ask a friend to tap the spoon on the string with another metal spoon.

3

The spoons sound like bells and the noise is very loud. Compare the noise they make when you hold the string away from your ears.

Speaking string

The Gruesome twins can talk to each other from the top of the house to the garden with their speaking string. You can do the same. All you need is a length of string with a plastic cup at both ends. Pull the string tight and don't let it touch anything. Whisper into the cup or hold it to your ear to listen.

You can make the string as long as you like, up to about 20 metres.

Attaching the cups

Make a small hole in the bottom of each cup. Push the end of the string through the hole and tie a knot in it.

What is happening?

The spoons sound like loud bells and your voice is heard far away on the speaking string because string is solid.

Sounds travel better and faster through solids and liquids than they do through air.

Hearing games

1

Don't put the pencil inside your ear.

Put a pencil to your ear and scratch the pencil lightly. The scratching sound travels along the solid pencil. See how loud it sounds.

2

When you go swimming, try making noises or talking to your friends under water. See how different voices and noises sound in water.

3

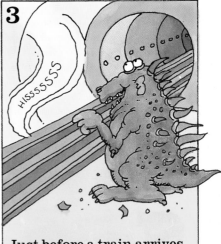

Just before a train arrives, listen to the rails hissing. The noise of the train travels along the solid rails faster than it does through the air.

Did you know?

Red Indians used to put their ears to the ground to listen for horses in the distance. They could hear the noise of galloping hooves in the ground before they could hear them coming through the air.

Come-back can

Micky is showing the monster gang his crazy come-back cans. He rolls them along the ground and they come back on their own, as if by magic. Try making one yourself. You may need some help.

THINGS YOU NEED

EMPTY CYLINDER-SHAPE CONTAINER WITH A LID. (about 15cm tall and 8cm wide)

THICK RUBBER BAND CUT TO MAKE A STRIP (about 15cm long)

SMALL STONE
PIECE OF CLING FILM
STRING

1 Make a hole in the bottom of the container and in the lid. Push the rubber band through the bottom hole and tie a knot at the end.

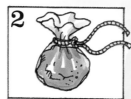

2 Wrap the stone in cling film and tie it with a piece of string about 15cm long, as shown above.

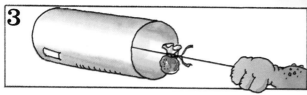

3 Pull the rubber band tight and tie the stone to the rubber band mid-way between each end. You may need help with this.

4 Thread the rubber band through the lid and tie a knot on the outside.

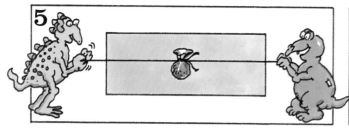

5 The rubber band should be pulled quite tight with the stone in the middle. To make final adjustments, pull the ends of the rubber band and tie new knots.

6 Try rolling your come-back can on a smooth flat surface. If it doesn't roll back, try tightening the rubber band or use a heavier stone.

You can race the cans with your friends.

How it works

As the container rolls along the floor, the stone makes the rubber band wind up. When it stops rolling, the rubber band unwinds and the container rolls backwards.

Crazy rollers

Micky and Clutty Putty have discovered two more crazy can rolling ideas. To try them you will need an empty tin can with a lid.

1. Micky's can

Stick a small lump of plasticine inside the can. Put on the lid and roll it along the floor.

2. Clutty's can

Fill the can with gravel or sand to just below the half-way mark. Push the lid on tight and try rolling it.

How the cans roll

Micky's can wobbles and rolls unevenly. The plasticine lump makes one side of the can heavier than the other.

Clutty Putty's can hardly rolls at all. The gravel or sand makes the bottom half of the can so heavy that it cannot roll round.

29

Further explanations

The explanations in this book are obviously highly simplified. The notes below are intended for those who wish to explain the activities in more detail, to older children.

Pages 6-7

These experiments produce a chemical reaction. Acids react with carbonates to give off carbon dioxide (CO_2). They may also produce other substances.

Pages 10-11

The idea of outward and inward forces is used to simplify the explanation of movement in a circle. A more detailed explanation is as follows:

When something moves in a circle, such as a spinning bucket, two forces are at work. The first is the one that makes it move, in other words, the pushing movement of your arm. This obeys the first law of motion which says that an object moves in a straight line unless another force acts upon it.

You can see this law in action if you spin a bucket, then let it go. The bucket flies off. It appears to fly outwards, but if you look closely you will see that it moves in a straight line, at a tangent to the circle of movement. This is what is meant by the simplified term, "outward force" (sometimes referred to as "centrifugal" force).

If you keep hold of the bucket, it does not move in a straight line, but spins round in a circle. This means a second force is acting on the bucket. It is centripetal force, meaning "seeking the centre" and it pulls inwards. When you spin a bucket, your arm is the centrepetal force as it stops the bucket flying away.

Aunty Mabel's salad spinner shows the two forces working very clearly. Your arm and the string handle act as the centripetal force to stop the container flying away. The container does the same thing for the water. Where there are holes in the container, there is no centripetal force to hold in the water. As a result, the water escapes from the container, flying at a tangent to the circle of movement.

Pages 12-13

Surface tension occurs because water molecules attract each other. The molecules at the surface have nothing to attract above them, so they pull extra hard at the sides. This produces a surface layer which acts rather like a skin.

Soap reduces the surface tension of the water by breaking down the forces of attraction between the water molecules. This happens because one end of a soap molecule (the "head") is attracted to water, while the other end (the "tail") repels it.

In the first experiment, the soapy straw breaks down the attraction of the molecules in the centre of the bowl. The molecules at the edge are still strong and so they pull the others towards them. This pulling action plus the pushing of the soap molecules moves the matches. Similarly, when soap touches a firm water droplet, the molecules stop pulling together and spread out.

Soapy water washes dirt away because of the action of the soap molecules. The tail sticks to dirt and grease while the head pulls towards the water. As this happens, the head pulls the tail, bringing the dirt away with it.

Pages 16-17

Everything is made up of tiny particles called atoms. These in turn contain even tinier particles which are charged with static electricity. There are two types: positive charges called protons and negative charges called electrons. Most of the time atoms are neutral or "uncharged" because they have an equal number of electrons and protons.

When two things are rubbed together, electrons sometimes move from one to the other. When this happens the objects are said to be charged with static electricity. The atoms in a charged object have an unequal number of protons and electrons. If there are more protons, it is positively charged. If there are more electrons, it is negatively charged.

Charges of electricity attract charges of the opposite type and repel those of the same type. In these experiments, charged objects attract things that are uncharged. This happens in the following way:

A rubbed balloon is negatively charged. The paper scraps are neutral. The negative charges on the balloon repel the negative charges in the paper, pushing them to the opposite end of the scrap. This leaves the positive charges close to the balloon. It is attracted to them and the paper scraps stick.

These experiments do not introduce the idea of negative and positive charges or repulsion of similar charges.

Pages 18-19

Action and reaction is another way of describing Newton's third law of motion. Newton's law states that for every force that acts, there is an equal and opposite force that reacts.

Pages 20-21

Scientists measure air pressure in millimetres of mercury. At sea level the pressure is 760mm of mercury. Three-quarters of the way up Mount Everest (5 miles above sea level), the pressure is 270mm of mercury.

Pages 26-27

The speed of sound in dry air at normal temperature and pressure is 331.4m (1087.3ft) per second. In sea water it travels at 1540m (5052.5ft) per second.

Results

Page 5: Crystals

Salt and sugar will dissolve in hot water. Sand and precious stones will not.

(If you tried this experiment with precious stones, Slimy Sid would like to know where you found them!)

Page 22: Density test

This chart shows the results for the density test when all the liquids, including the water, are the same temperature.

Fruit cordial Treacle Maple syrup	These sink. They are denser than water.
Cooking oil	This floats. It is less dense than water.
Milk Orange juice	These mix with water. This means they have more or less the same density as water.*

*Milk and orange juice may sink before mixing if they are colder than the water. If they are warmer, they may float before they mix.

Making a science kit

You can build up your own kit of science equipment and from everyday things that you find at home. The list below shows some useful things to look out for.

Balloons
Bottles
Cellophane (Look out for coloured sweet wrappings.)
Cans and tins with lids
Cardboard
Containers, such as ice cream tubs and yoghurt pots
Corks
Funnel
Jam jars
Jug
Magnet
Mirror (pocket size)
Paper
Rubber bands
Scissors
Spoons
Straws
String
Tubes (You can find these inside rolls of paper towels.)

Printed in Belgium

SCIENCE TRICKS & MAGIC

Contents Part 2

About this section

In this section there are lots of science tricks for you to try on your friends. There are also fun experiments with strange results that make science seem like magic.

All the experiments are completely safe.

Some experiments are messy.

Try out your tricks on a willing volunteer.

Some experiments are noisy.

You may need a grown up to help you with a few experiments.

The monster gang have tried out every experiment. This picture shows some of the monsters at work.

Doing the experiments

The puzzle answers are on page 63.

The monsters show you how to do each experiment in easy step-by-step instructions.

You can find out how and why each experiment works. The scientific ideas behind each one are explained.★

There are ideas for further experiments to try and several science puzzles to solve.

Equipment and ingredients

All the experiments use ordinary, everyday equipment. You can probably find most of the ingredients at home. If not, you should be able to buy them at a local supermarket.

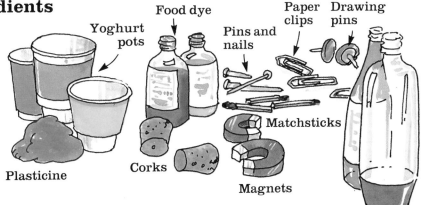

Yoghurt pots

Food dye

Pins and nails

Paper clips

Drawing pins

Matchsticks

Plasticine

Corks

Magnets

Plastic bottles

It's a good idea to start collecting a science kit. Here are some things you may find useful.

★There are some extra, more detailed explanations on page 62.

Funny feelings

Snivel is doing some strange tests on his friends. He wants to find out how they feel things.

Find a willing test victim, and you can try them too. Compare your results with Snivel's.

The tweezer test

1

2 In some places Grummit can feel both prongs. In other places they feel like one.

3

4 Grummit's hands, especially his fingertips, are very sensitive.

I can feel 2 prongs.

First, Snivel blindfolds his friend Grummit to make sure he can't see anything.

He touches Grummit with a pair of tweezers (sometimes with 1 prong, sometimes with 2 prongs) and asks how many he can feel each time.

He marks each touch on a map of Grummit's body. Red dots stand for correct answers, blue dots for wrong answers.

Grummit's skin is most sensitive to touch in the places where he is able to feel 2 prongs.

How sensitive are your feet?

Many people, and all monsters, have very ticklish feet. But feet are not sensitive in the same way as fingertips. Try the tweezer test on the soles of your feet.

Snivel's touch detective game

The sensitive parts of your body are the parts with the best sense of touch. You can see this in Snivel's touch detective game.

First Snivel collects several different objects with varied shapes and surfaces.

He blindfolds Clutty Putty. She feels each object with her feet and tries to work out what it is.

Try it yourself – it's quite tricky. Then touch each object with your hands. See how much easier it is.

Feeling cold

Snivel is very very cold. He can't feel his fingertips and he is having problems doing up the zip of his ski suit.

He reckons that the cold has affected his sense of touch. Find out if he is right by trying the tests on the right.

Pinch-me test

Make one hand very cold. You could tie it to a bag of frozen peas or put it in a bowl of ice-cubes for a few minutes.

Ask someone to pinch one finger on each hand. Which one hurts most? Fumble's warm finger hurts much more than the cold one.

Pin test

Try picking up a pin with your cold hand. Fumble finds it very hard. The cold makes it difficult to feel the pin properly.

Eye tricks

Sometimes your eyes play tricks on you. They see things that are not really true. These are called optical illusions.

Look at the picture on the right. Slimy Sid thinks the red lines are curved. Is he correct?

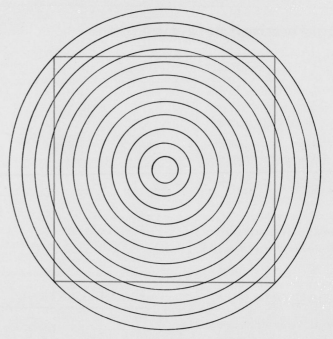

If you put a ruler along the red lines, you will see they are straight. Your eyes are fooled by the black circles which make the red lines seem curved.

Eye-teasers

Look first, then check what you see with a ruler. Did your eyes trick you?

Is the blue line longer than the green line, or are they the same length?

Are the green lines the same length or is the top one longer?

Are the red lines parallel? (Parallel lines are the same distance apart, all the way along.)

38

Colour confusion

Colours can also fool your eyes. Light, bright colours can appear bigger than dark, dull colours. Light, bright colours reflect light whereas dark, dull colours swallow up or "absorb" light. Try the colour trick, below, on your friends.

1 Draw round a glass to make a circle shape.

2 The yellow circle looks bigger. In fact they are the same size.

3 Which circle looks bigger?

Cut out 2 paper circles exactly the same size. Paint one circle yellow and the other one dark brown.

Stick the circles on a wall.* Tell your friends to go to the other end of the room. Ask them which circle looks bigger.

Try the experiment again with other colours. You will probably find that light, bright colours seem larger than dark, dull ones.

Coloured clothes

Some monsters think that dark colours make them look thin and light colours make them look fat.

Look around you and see if you think this is true.

*Check with a grown up first to make sure you don't damage the wall.

Magic bean stalks

The Gruesome twins have discovered that they can grow amazing plants from ordinary beans and seeds used for cooking and eating.

This picture shows some of the things they grew. They found everything in their kitchen cupboard.

Spice and herb seeds such as coriander, fennel and mustard seeds.

Dried peas and beans, such as kidney beans and butter beans.

Look for some beans and seeds in your own kitchen. You can find out how to grow them below.

How to grow seeds

Label each yoghurt pot.

Fester soaks the dried peas and beans in a bowl of water overnight. Then he buries them in yoghurt pots filled with soil. Blot sprinkles some of the small seeds on damp cotton wool. He plants others about a fingernail deep in soil. They keep the soil and cotton wool damp and wait to see what will happen.

Some seeds grow tiny shoots in a day or two. Others grow very slowly and a few don't sprout at all. See what happens to your seeds.

40

Things to try

Some vegetables contain seeds. Try planting some.

Fester and Blot are having a fruit feast. As they eat the fruit, they plant the pips and stones. Try doing this yourself.

Slimy Sid is planting hamster food and bird seed. Aunty Mabel thinks he is silly. What do you think? Try it and see.

How seeds grow

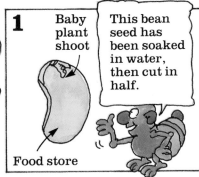

1 Baby plant shoot

This bean seed has been soaked in water, then cut in half.

Food store

A seed contains the beginnings of a baby plant and a store of food for the plant to use as it starts to grow.

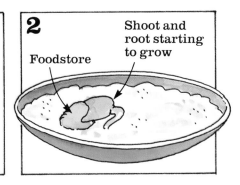

2 Shoot and root starting to grow

Foodstore

You can grow a seed on cotton wool because it has its own food store. Later the plant will make its own food.

3

A seed needs warmth and moisture to make it grow. Some seeds need a lot of warmth to start growing.

Did you know?

If seeds are kept dry, they will keep for ages without growing. In the desert, seeds lie in the ground until there is enough water to make them grow. After a rainfall lots of desert flowers appear.

4

If your seeds will not grow, try putting them in a warm place, such as an airing cupboard.*

*Some seeds and beans that are meant for eating are treated to stop them growing.

Freaky flowers

You can fool your friends with freaky coloured flowers, just like Slimy Sid's blue and green carnations.

To do this you will need a jar, food dye, water and white flowers such as carnations.

How to do it

1

Pour some water and several drops of food dye into the bottom of a jar. Put the flowers in the jar.

2

1 DAY   3 DAYS

After a day or so, you will see flecks of colour on the tips of the petals. In about 2 or 3 days the flowers change colour completely.

Why do the flowers change colour?

Short-stemmed flowers change colour faster than long-stemmed flowers. Can you guess why? Check your answer on page 63.

Flowers suck up water through their stems into their leaves and petals. You can't usually see this, but food dye shows through white petals.

Plants in the soil

Plants suck up water from the soil through their roots and stems. The water contains minerals which the plants use to make food.

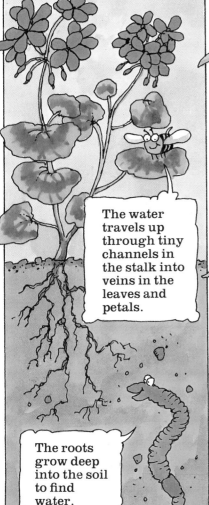

The water travels up through tiny channels in the stalk into veins in the leaves and petals.

The roots grow deep into the soil to find water.

Grummit's silly celery experiment

In some plants, such as celery, you can see the veins that carry water quite clearly. Try Grummit's silly celery experiment.

1

Grummit's assistant fills the bottom of a jar with water coloured with food dye. Grummit puts a stick of celery into the jar.

2

Grummit checks the celery every hour or so to watch the coloured water creeping up the veins in the celery. His assistant makes a note of its progress.

3

Grummit cuts the celery into slices to see the veins more clearly. The spots of colour show the ends of the veins.

Cooking magic

Snivel is doing some cooking. He is turning eggs, sugar and a little food dye into monstrous blue meringues.

The monster gang think it might be magic, but Snivel says it is science. Follow Snivel's recipe and see what you think.

Is it magic?

$2\frac{1}{2}$ hours later, the gooey swirls have turned into crisp meringues. Find out how this happens, below.

When you whisk egg whites, hundreds of tiny air bubbles get trapped and make a stiff foam.

The oven's heat makes the air bubbles "expand" and the foam puffs up. It also causes a chemical change in the egg white making it solid. This is called "coagulation".

1

Snivel asks Aunty Mabel to turn on the oven to gas mark $\frac{1}{4}$ (110°C or 225°F).

2

This is quite tricky

He separates the whites from the yolks of 4 eggs. You can ask a grown-up to help you do this.

3

He whisks the egg whites in a big bowl. First they go fluffy, then they go stiff and white.

4

When the egg white is stiff, Snivel adds 220g (8oz) of caster sugar and stirs it in very very gently. Weedle adds a few drops of food dye.

5

He drops spoonfuls of the mixture in round, swirly shapes on to greased baking trays. He puts them in the oven for $2\frac{1}{2}$ hours.

Cooking cake mixture

The heat in an oven turns a sticky mixture of butter, sugar, eggs and flour into a cake.

The heat dries out some of the liquid in the mixture.

Heat hardens a substance called gluten in the flour and turns the egg white solid.

Tiny air bubbles in the cake mixture expand. This makes the cake "rise" and gives it a light and fluffy texture.

Deadeye Dick's dreadful disaster

My cake is flat.

Deadeye Dick's cake is a disaster. It hasn't risen. He followed the recipe correctly, but he kept opening the oven door while it was cooking. Can you guess what went wrong? Check your answer on page 63.

More about eggs

Ask a grown-up to help you poach or fry an egg. Watch it coagulate (turn from a liquid into a solid). Which part of the egg goes solid first?

In a very hot climate, eggs can coagulate in the heat of the sun.

Tricks with shadows

The monster gang are enthralled by Deadeye Dick's Magical Shadow Show. Follow what they are doing in the picture on the right, and you can make a shadow show too.

For moving puppets, make shapes with your hands.

For the screen, you can use a white wall or white paper stuck to a pinboard.

You need a powerful torch with a bright beam.

The room should be completely dark.

To make shadow puppets, cut shapes and figures out of card and stick them to long, thin sticks.

Scary shadows

On dark and eerie nights, Slimy Sid scares his friends with spooky shadows at the windows. You can find out how he does it, below.

1 First he sticks white paper onto the outside of a window. He stands back and shines a torch on it.

2 Then his assistant makes monstrous, scary movements in front of the torch's beam.

3 Inside, in the dark, the monsters see a spooky shadow moving against a ghostly, light window.

How shadows are made

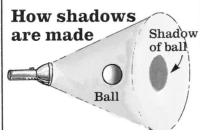

Shadow of ball

Ball

Shadows are made when light is blocked by an object. Light travels in lots of straight lines called rays. Light rays cannot bend round things that get in their way. Objects that block light are said to be "opaque".

Making shadows bigger

Bring the torch closer to the object. It blocks more light, so its shadow is bigger.

Making shadows smaller

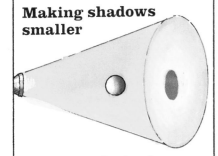

Now move the torch away. The shadow gets smaller because it blocks less of the torch's beam.

Mystery shadows

Transparent (see-through) objects cast only very faint shadows. This is because most of the light rays can travel through them. Snivel is making some weird, mystery shadows with transparent objects.

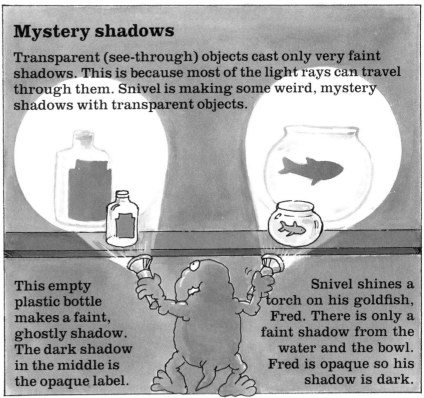

This empty plastic bottle makes a faint, ghostly shadow. The dark shadow in the middle is the opaque label.

Snivel shines a torch on his goldfish, Fred. There is only a faint shadow from the water and the bowl. Fred is opaque so his shadow is dark.

Shadow puzzle

Grummit is at the monster cup final (Monster Gang Utd v Reptile Rangers). He can't work out why each player has 4 shadows. Can you? Check your answer on page 63.

47

Magical magnets

Magnets have a strange power. They pull things towards them, as if by magic.

You can find out about magnets and this peculiar power below. Then try some of the monsters' favourite magnet tricks and games, on the right.

Bar magnets

Horseshoe magnets

These magnets come from the inside of old loudspeakers.

These are fun magnets for sticking onto metal surfaces.

Magnets come in all sorts of shapes and sizes. You can buy them in toy shops, hardware shops and department stores.

To find out if something is magnetic, hold a magnet close to it.

Magnets pull or "attract" most (but not all) metal things. When something is attracted by a magnet it is said to be magnetic.

The pull of the magnet is strongest at its ends.

You can feel the pull of a magnet when you hold a nail or pin close to it. Which part of the magnet pulls hardest?

Some magnets have a stronger pulling force than others.

Slimy Sid's magnetic mini-monsters

Slimy Sid terrifies his Aunty Mabel with his magnetic mini-monsters. You can make your friends squeal and squirm too. Find out how on the right.

Magnet puzzles

See if you can solve these two puzzles. You can check your solutions on page 63.

Can you remove a paper clip from a glass of water? You can't put anything in the glass nor can you tip out the water.

Slimy Sid has dropped Aunty Mabel's pins and plastic buttons. He has 30 seconds to sort them out and pick them up. How can he do it?

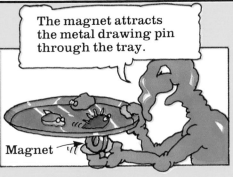

The magnet attracts the metal drawing pin through the tray.

Magnet

Make a small monster shape out of plasticine or clay. Stick a drawing pin into the bottom.

Put the monster on a tray and hold a magnet under it, below the monster. Move the magnet and the monster should move too.*

If you attach a magnet to a long stick, you can control your monster from a distance.

Sharks and shrimps

Try playing Sharks and Shrimps. Cut out lots of paper shrimps and 6 paper sharks. Attach a paper clip to each one and put them in a box.

Shark   Shrimp

The players fish for shrimps with a magnet tied to a piece of string. The winner is the one to catch the most shrimps. If you catch a shark, you're out.

More about magnets

The ends of a magnet are called poles. One is a north pole, the other a south pole. If you have two magnets, try holding the ends together.

If the ends pull together it means one is a north pole and other is a south pole.

If they push away or "repel" each other, it means they are both the same type.

Something to try

If you float a bar magnet in a bowl of water, one end will point to the North. This is why the ends of a magnet are called north and south poles.

Float the magnet in a plastic container.

*If the monster doesn't move very well, try a stronger magnet or a thinner tray.

49

Disappearing tricks

Deadeye Dick has discovered a way of making things disappear. To try out his tricks you need a colour viewer. Find out how to make one on the right.

You could use a cellophane sweet wrapper, like this.

1 Find a piece of yellow cellophane or clear yellow plastic.

2 Cut out a card frame, just bigger than the cellophane.

3 Stick the cellophane to the frame with glue or sticky tape.

Vanishing windows

Why the windows disappear

The yellow viewer makes the white walls look yellow. The yellow windows do not show up against the walls and so they "disappear".

Some of the windows have disappeared! Now there are only 17.

This is a picture of Pessky Mo's new igloo. There are 21 windows. Look at the igloo through your yellow viewer and count the number of windows again.

Try making a red viewer. Look at the picture again. How many windows are there now?

50

Magical mystery message

Copy this message on to a sheet of white paper. Write the ringed letters in yellow and each of the others in a different colour. Read the message through your yellow viewer.

NO (SMOKING)(IS) ALLOWED IN THE (T)RAIN

The yellow letters should disappear and change the messsage.

Perhaps you can invent some mystery messages of your own.

How colour viewers work

Light looks colourless, but really it is made up of different colours. You can sometimes see these colours in rainbows.

A colour viewer separates or "filters" the colours in light. It only lets light the same colour as itself travel through it.

Try looking through different colour viewers.

Colour viewers, or filters, make white things appear the same colour as themselves, but they can also change other colours.

Snivel's red viewer only lets through red light. Slimy Sid's white bow tie look red, but his green body looks black!

Slimy Sid's car crash puzzle

Slimy Sid has just had an unfortunate collision with a monster-police car. He says he didn't see the red light. Can you work out why? Check your answer on page 63.

51

Musical magic

The monster gang are making magic musical sounds with everyday objects. Try doing this yourself.

Try making sounds with other ordinary things you find about the house, too.

Tap a blunt table knife. Listen to the humming sound it makes.

Wobble a large piece of stiff cardboard backwards and forwards.

Hang a saucepan lid or knives and forks on a string. Tap them with a metal spoon.

Gently rub a damp finger round and round the rim of a wine glass. It should produce a strange singing sound.

Ask a grown up to bend a saw backwards and forwards. It makes an almost spooky sound. Don't try this yourself.

How sounds are made

All sounds are caused by shaking movements called vibrations.

Ordinary everyday objects produce sounds when they are made to vibrate.

You can see the blade vibrating in a blur of movement.

When an object vibrates it makes the air around it vibrate as well. The vibrations travel

You can't see air vibrating.

through the air. Your ear drum shakes with the vibration and you hear a sound.

Changing speed

You can make a sound higher or lower by changing the speed or "frequency" of a vibration. A fast vibration makes a high note. A slow vibration makes a low note.

You can test this out by wobbling a piece of card at different speeds.

Try plucking a rubber band. Then stretch it and pluck it again. It vibrates more quickly when it is stretched and the plucking sound is higher.

Slimy Sid's piano trick

Slimy Sid sings a note into the open top of the piano and presses the loud pedal (the one on the right). The monster gang are amazed. The piano "sings" the same note back to him, as if by magic. If you have a piano, you can try it yourself.

What is happening?

The piano string that makes the same note as Slimy Sid vibrates in sympathy. This is called resonance.

Aunty Mabel's singing wine glass

Aunty Mabel is trying to make a wine glass resonate. Follow what she does and try it yourself.

1 Aunty Mabel pings a wine glass with her nail to find out what note it makes.

2 Then she tries to sing the same note. If she succeeds, the glass should resonate.

3 It is very hard to do this.

If her voice is loud enough, the glass could vibrate so much that it cracks.

Clutty Putty's purple potion

The monster gang are puzzled by Clutty Putty's purple potion. When it mixes with another ingredient it changes colour, as if by magic.

You can discover the secret of how and why it works on the opposite page. First find out how to make it, below.

How to make the potion

1

Chop up half a red cabbage. Put the pieces in a saucepan and cover them with cold water.

2

Put the saucepan on the stove and let it boil for 5 minutes. Ask a grown up to help you do this.

3

When it is cool, separate the cabbage and the liquid by straining it through a sieve.*

Colour changes

Clutty puts a little purple potion in the bottom of 2 small jars. She pours a teaspoon of vinegar into the jar on the left and a teaspoon of baking powder into the jar on the right.

Almost immediately the liquid changes colour. In the jar on the left, the potion turns pink, on the right it turns green.

*You need the liquid, not the cabbage bits. You can eat these if you like.

Why the potion changes colour

The purple potion is an indicator. It changes colour when it mixes with an acid or an alkali. These are names scientists use to describe and group substances.

Vinegar is an acid. It turns the potion pink. Baking powder is an alkali and it turns the potion green.

Milk   Fizzy cola   Lime juice

Tooth paste

Washing soda

Yoghurt

Salt   Soap

Lemon juice

Baking powder

Black tea

You can record the results of each test in a notebook.

Lime juice   Green   Acid

Here are some everyday acid and alkali substances. See if you can sort out the acids from the alkalis. Follow what Snivel does on the right.

Snivel puts some of each substance into a little purple potion. Acids turn the potion red or pink. Alkalis turn the potion green or blue.

Mixing acids with alkalis

Guess what happens to the purple potion if you mix it with an acid and an alkali at the same time. Try it and see.

Mix a little lemon juice (acid) with some purple potion and it should turn pink. Add some washing soda (alkali) to the mixture. It should turn back to purple. This means that the mixture is neither acid nor alkali. In other words, it is neutral.

Did you know?

Bee sting poison is acid. You can soothe bee stings by rubbing them with bicarbonate of soda (an alkali).

Balancing tricks

Have you ever tried walking along a narrow wall or plank with your arms pinned to your sides? This is what the monsters are trying to do. It's very tricky. Try it yourself.

If your hands leave the side of your body, you must start again.

It is much easier to walk with your arms stretched out. You balance more easily because your body makes a wider shape and your weight is spread out over your feet.

More about balancing

When something balances, it is said to be stable. This means it is hard to topple over. Low things with a wide base are more stable than tall things with a narrow base.

Some of these objects are more stable than others. Which are they? Try knocking them over to find out.

Making things stable

You can make something more stable by giving it a broader base. Try sticking a piece of card to the bottom of a cardboard tube. It is more difficult to push over.

Another way of making something more stable it to make its base heavier. Pour some water into a plastic bottle. It should topple over less easily.

Balancing puzzles

Aunty Mabel's automobile

Blot's buggy

Snivel's speed machine

Which of these monster vehicles is the most stable? You can check your answer on page 63.

Which boat is more likely to topple over and capsize?

Balancing potato monster

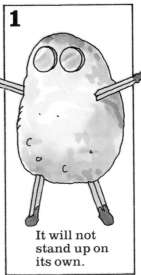

1 It will not stand up on its own.

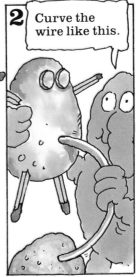

2 Curve the wire like this.

3

Make a monster out of a knobbly potato. Give it matchstick arms and legs and drawing pin eyes.

Stick a length of stiff wire into the potato. Attach another, larger potato to the other end.

Put the monster on a shelf and it should balance, wobbling backwards and forwards.

How does it balance?

The potato monster balances because the greatest part of its weight (the second potato) comes below the point where it balances (its matchstick feet).

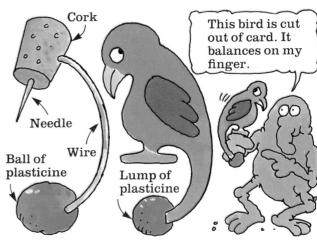

Cork

Needle

Ball of plasticine

Wire

Lump of plasticine

This bird is cut out of card. It balances on my finger.

These toys balance in the same way. Try making them.

Tricky reflections

A reflection is what you see when you look in a mirror. You can also see reflections in water, windows and other shiny surfaces.

Like most monster magicians, Slimy Sid uses reflections to create special effects. Try his finger in the flame trick, on the right.

1 To set the trick up, Slimy Sid puts a lighted candle in front of a window. The flame is reflected in the window.

Flame's reflection
Flame

2 He goes outside with an unlit candle. Weedle tells him where to stand so the unlit candle appears below the reflection.

Unlit candle

3 Slimy Sid puts his finger on the unlit candle wick. The monsters come into the room and see his finger in the flame!

Slimy Sid's Super Snooper

Slimy Sid's Super Snooper uses mirrors to peep round corners and spy over the fence. Try making one yourself.

Things you need

Piece of card 55cm (22in) long and 35cm (14in) wide, 2 pocket mirrors about 9cm (3½in) long and 6cm (2½in) wide, scissors, glue and sticky tape.

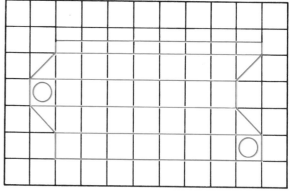

Draw lines on the card to make a grid, as shown above. Space the lines exactly 5cm (2in) apart. Copy the red and green lines and the red circles on to your grid.

Mirror tricks

You can do strange tricks with mirrors because reflections show things back to front.

Lopside Ed's reflection is different from his passport photo.

Put a patch over your left eye. Look at your reflection. Which eye is covered?

Try holding this book in front of the mirror. Why can't you read it?

Car puzzle

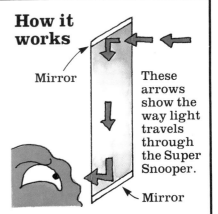

Slimy Sid has copied the monster ambulance by painting a back to front sign on his car. Do you know why?*

2

Cut around the red lines. Then cut out the red circles to make two holes.

3

Fold the card on the green lines to make a square tube. Stick down the flap.

4

Mirror

Attach a mirror (reflective side facing inwards) to each end of the tube.

How it works

Mirror

Mirror

These arrows show the way light travels through the Super Snooper.

The mirror at the top reflects light down the tube. The mirror at the bottom reflects the light into your eye.

---

*You can find out on page 63.   59

Sinking and floating

Deadeye Dick has promised a trip on his racing raft to the first monster who can make a lump of plasticine float.

The monster gang are not having much luck. See if you can do it. There are some clues about how things float, below.

How things float

1

2

3 You can feel upthrust in a swimming pool. Stretch out your arms and they float upwards.

4

When you put something in water, some of the water is pushed aside, or "displaced". Slimy Sid's bath overflows because his body displaces the water.

Big things displace more water than small things. Ugly Mug has a bigger body than Slimy Sid, so he displaces more water.

When water is displaced, a force called "upthrust" pushes upwards. The amount of upthrust depends on how much water is displaced.

This plasticine lump sinks. It is quite heavy but it is small and doesn't displace much water. This means there is not enough upthrust to make it float.

Slimy Sid's magic egg trick

Slimy Sid puts an egg into a jar filled with water. It sinks.

He puts the same egg into another jar. Magically, it floats.

How the trick works

To make salty water, stir about 8 tablespoons of salt into ½ litre (1 pint) of hot water.

The jars contain different types of water. Different types of water have different amounts of upthrust. The jar on the left contains tap water.

The jar on the right contains very salty water. This has more upthrust than tap water, so things float in it more easily.

Did you know?

On the high seas

On Reptile River

There is more upthrust in sea water than there is in river water. This means that Deadeye Dick's pirate ship, the Jolly Dodger, floats higher in the salty sea than it does on the Reptile River.

5

Mould the plasticine into a bowl shape. It is still as heavy as the lump, but it is bigger and displaces more water. This means there is more upthrust and it floats.

Further explanations

The explanations in this book are obviously highly simplified. The notes below are intended for those who wish to explain the activities in more detail, to older children.

Pages 48-49

Magnets attract iron and steel and alloys that contain these metals. Magnets do not point to the geographical north pole. Instead, they point to a position in Northern Canada called the magnetic north pole.

Pages 50-51

Light is made up of a mixture of colours. These are commonly divided into 7 colours of the spectrum: red, orange, yellow, green, blue, indigo and violet.

Objects appear coloured because of the colour of light they reflect. For instance, a red object reflects red light, but it absorbs all the other colours. A white object reflects all the colours of light. A black object absorbs them.

A colour filter allows light the same colour as itself to pass through it. For instance, a green filter permits green light to pass through it but it blocks other colours. If you look at a red object through a green filter, its red light is blocked. No light passes through the filter and so the object appears black.

There are three primary colours of light: red, green and blue. Other colours are a mixture of these. They act differently to coloured paints. For instance, green and red paint make brown, but green and red light make yellow.

If you look at a yellow object through a green filter, it appears green. This happens because the red light reflected by the yellow object is blocked, but the green light is allowed through.

Pages 52-53

Vibrations force the surrounding air to vibrate by pushing the air molecules together, forming a compression. The compression is passed on through the air in a wave.

The pitch of a sound depends on how frequent vibrations are. The number of vibrations made in 1 second is called frequency and is measured in Hertz (Hz). The human ear can usually hear sounds with frequencies between 20 vibrations per second (20Hz) and 20,000 vibrations per second (20kHz).

Pages 54-55

Clutty Putty's purple potion is a well known home-made indicator. An indicator is used to show the presence of acid or alkali in a substance.

Chemists use a range of numbers (called pH numbers) to measure levels of acidity and alkalinity. Acids range from 1 to 6, alkalis from 8 to 14 and 7 is neutral.

Pages 56-57

Balance depends on the pull of the earth's gravity. Gravity pulls downwards on every particle of an object with a force that is equal to the weight of the particle. At the same time, there is a point where the whole weight of an object seems to act and it balances. This is called the centre of gravity.

Stable objects have a low centre of gravity: the lower the centre of gravity, the greater the stability. The centre of gravity can by lowered by widening the base or increasing the weight of the base.

An object always tries to move until its centre of gravity is as low as possible. In other words it will topple over. This is what happens if you try to balance a pencil on its point.

An object topples over when its centre of gravity moves outside its base. This explains why it is difficult to walk along a narrow wall with your arms pinned to your sides. If you hold your arms out and move them up and down, you can alter your centre of gravity to keep it above, not outside, your base (your feet).

Pages 58-59

A light ray reflects or bounces off a plane (flat) mirror at the same angle as it hits it.

Slimy Sid's super snooper is a periscope. The mirrors are tilted at 45°. The light rays hit the first mirror at 45° and bounce off at the same angle. This means they effectively turn a corner to travel at right angles down the tube. The same thing happens at the second mirror, but in the opposite direction. The light rays hit the mirror at 45° and bounce off at the same angle, out of the periscope into your eye.

Pages 60-61

The amount of upthrust on an object in a liquid is equal to the weight of the liquid the object displaces. An object displaces the same volume of liquid in salt water as it does in fresh water. But salt water is denser (heavier) than fresh water. This means the upthrust in salt water is greater.

Puzzle answers

Page 42

Short-stemmed flowers change colour more quickly because the coloured water has less distance to travel to the petals.

Page 45

Deadeye Dick's cake is flat because he opened the oven door while it was cooking. This let cold air into the oven which stopped the air bubbles puffing up, or expanding.

Page 47

The players have 4 shadows because of the floodlights. There are 4 sets of floodlights, one in each corner of the pitch. Each set casts a separate shadow.

Page 48

1. Hold a magnet under the glass, then slide it gently up the side. The magnet should be strong enough to pull the paper clip with it.
2. Slimy Sid should hold a magnet over the pins and buttons. The magnet will pick up the metal pins but not the plastic buttons. (He will have to pick up the buttons by hand.)

Page 51

The green lenses in Slimy Sid's glasses only let through green light. They block the colour of the red traffic light. To Slimy Sid, the red light would look black.

Page 57

1. Snivel's speed machine is the most stable. It has a wide base and the weight is low.
2. The Slime family are standing up which makes their boat top heavy and likely to capsize. Deadeye Dick's boat is more stable. He is sitting down which keeps the weight in the boat low.

Page 59

The sign on Slimy Sid's car will read correctly when the driver in front looks into the rear-view mirror, attached to the windscreen.

Ambulances use back to front signs to tell drivers what sort of vehicle is coming up behind. A driver reads the word AMBULANCE and gets out of the way in an emergency.

Index

First published in 1985 by Usborne Publishing Ltd, 20 Garrick Street, London WC2E 9BJ, England.

© 1985 Usborne Publishing Ltd.

The name Usborne and the device 🐝 are the Trade Marks of Usborne Publishing Ltd.

Printed in Belgium.